GET PAID

GET PAID

10 SECRETS TO A PROFITABLE BUSINESS

Kimberly M. Walker

Catalyst Coaching & Consulting

www.TheCoachKim.com

Get Paid: 10 Secrets to a Profitable Business

Copyright © 2015 by Kimberly M. Walker
Published by Catalyst Coaching & Consulting
Staten Island, NY 10302
www.TheCoachKim.com

Requests for information should be addressed to:

Catalyst Coaching & Consulting
PO Box 20440
Staten Island, NY 10302
Info@TheCoachKim.com

ISBN: 0692563334
ISBN 13: 9780692563335
Library of Congress Control Number: 2015955814
Catalyst Coaching & Consulting, Staten Island, NY

TABLE OF CONTENTS

DEDICATION

*To you, the entrepreneur who is ready for the next level,
and wants to KIM - Keep It Moving!*

ACKNOWLEDGEMENTS

I am most grateful for all of the opportunities I have been afforded by my Heavenly Father.

A special thanks to my children, Joshua and Sara, who are entrepreneurs in their own right and my reason for wanting to pave the way and set an example. I love you to life!

My mother, Ollie, who taught me that I could do anything I set my mind to do. She was right all along.

Rev. Ann, my other mother, mentor, intercessor, and friend. Words cannot express my gratitude for your input in my life. Now it's your turn.

Angela, your prayers and our endless conversations caused me to dream again. Dreams do come true!

Ruth and Marcel, who have always been in my amen corner and encouraged me to "write the book."

My brother in Christ and fellow coach, David, who pushed me to "Get it done". The best is yet to come!

Free Gift for You

Congratulations on investing in your future! Not everyone who wants to "get paid" is willing to put in the effort. I believe in your success and want to further support you. Accordingly, I've created a special online treasure trove that will help you to increase your profits and grow faster, better and stronger.

These valuable gifts are available for a short time so please take advantage of them immediately. We reserve the right to withdraw this offer at any time.

To gain instant access, register your book now by going to www.TheCoachKim.com/Success-Tools. Your case sensitive password is:

CoachKim

Once you've registered, you'll get immediate access to:

Bonus #1 - 1-on-1 Personalized Laser Coaching Strategy Session with Coach Kim

Because of your new relationship with Coach Kim, you and your business are eligible to receive a complimentary coaching session valued at $175.

You will work one-on-one with your certified life and business coach, Coach Kim, to discover methods for overcoming obstacles, increasing your profits, and improving your quality of life.

Bonus #2 - Business Success Toolkit

Download your own toolkit of worksheets and resources. I personally used these resources to grow my business and others. These worksheets and resources include:

- CoachAbility Index Assessment
- Parallel Possibilities Worksheet
- Residual Income Worksheet
- Quick Hit Worksheet
- …and more!

INTRODUCTION

Anyone who knows me knows that I am an avid reader and teacher. The only thing I am more passionate about in my business life is helping others reach their full potential and transfer their knowledge. It is one of the reasons I choose to educate myself consistently and challenge myself to grow personally and professionally. In helping my small business clients grow their businesses and make more money, I began to see a common theme emerge that frustrated me to no end. No matter how big or small the business was, the main issues that prevented their success were the same. Most times, however, they failed to see the true issue, thinking instead that more marketing or another one-day sale would do the trick. I knew something had to change, and I set about to do just that.

In my experience, most of the clients I had the privilege to work with were masters at their craft and experts in their own right. The quality of their work spoke for itself and it was the draw for most of their customer relationships. Everyone wants to work with the expert, the highly knowledgeable and seasoned practitioner. They were also making some money but knew they had more profit-making potential than they were presently experiencing.

Most of them shared this one thing in common; they lacked the business skills to build and sustain a foundation for their success. They knew how to do what they do, whether that was construction, apparel sales, or childcare. However, they did not have the business savvy to build a platform for business success.

They were also too busy to stop and earn a business degree. They needed to learn by what I call the "grow and go" method. They needed to do it rather than spend days reading about it. They needed bite-sized instruction that they could implement readily while they actively ran their businesses. I have taught my clients and students that their business is the answer to someone else's needs and prayers. This book is the answer to theirs.

With quick, easy-to-read-and-implement entries, *Get Paid: 10 Secrets to a Profitable Business* will give you the nuggets you need to begin to build a foundation for your business success. Several books and workshops are in the works in the areas of business and life coaching for entrepreneurs.

It is with love and gratitude that I bring this to you, the entrepreneur who knows there is more ahead and they're willing to take a step and **KIM - Keep It Moving**!

Let's go!

SECRET #1

KNOW YOUR IDEAL CLIENT

One of the biggest mistakes that most entrepreneurs make is not taking enough time to get to know their ideal client. As an entrepreneur, the more you understand your ideal client, then the better you can serve them. It will also be easier to reach them, capture their business and retain it. The best thing you can do for your business and the quickest way to make a profit is to have an intimate knowledge of your ideal client.

For example, if you are a shoe salesman, who are your ideal clients? Is it really people with feet? Well that is 99.9 percent of the population save a few with special needs. That is too broad of an audience. I have a three-generational household, which includes my elderly mom, my adult son, and my college age daughter. All four of us wear shoes. However, none of us wear the same type of shoes and none of us shop in the same store for our shoes. We value different aspects of shoes when we go shopping for them. What appeals to my mother will not appeal to my daughter. The type of shoes my son purchases are not the same as those I purchase. Let's take this a step further.

How you market to the three different generations is also vastly dissimilar. My mother still gets the newspaper delivered to her front door and it is a perfect place to put an advertisement and a coupon, which she will take into a brick and mortar store. My children will search for what they want on their mobile devices and order online. I tend to use my laptop or tablet to see if it is available at a location near me. Consequently, if you market to my children in the newspaper that my mother reads, you will never reach them. Likewise, if you place a clickable ad online for my mother it will go completely unnoticed. I hope you can begin to see why understanding your ideal client is so valuable and why doing so will not only save you time and money, but it will also save you countless hours of frustration. Knowing who they are and what makes them tick will help you to market more effectively and increase your profits. Here are some questions to consider when identifying your ideal client:

- Who are they? Specify gender, age, employment status, and income level at the very least. Having a clear understanding of these demographics (statistical data of your ideal client) will help you to price properly and choose appealing colors for your marketing materials and website. Understanding key demographics will help you to know which marketing mediums will be most effective, including which keywords to use. This basic information is invaluable and will inform every aspect of your business.

- What problem do they desperately want to solve? What are they scouring the Internet for when looking for a solution? People will pay to stop pain or start pleasure. When you understand their pain and pleasure points you can customize products or services specifically designed for them. What pleasure do they want to experience? What pain do they want to stop?

- Where do they get their information? The medium from which they receive their news and information is the medium you should use to reach them. If they tend to get most of their information online, then that's where you should market to them. If not, find out where they are, and you should be there too.

- What type of electronic gadgets do they use? How technology savvy are they? If they love the latest and greatest technology, then your website and marketing should reflect that aspect of their nature. If not, you will focus less of your resources in this aspect of your business.

- What social media platforms do they frequent? At the time of is writing, there are over 1 billion people on Facebook. Chances are there is a portion of your target market there as well. However, if your ideal client is under 25, Instagram is a crowd favorite. If they are crafty or artsy, check out Pinterest. If they are business minded, LinkedIn is the way to go. Understanding this part of your ideal client's lifestyle will make your social media campaign much more effective.

- Where do they live? Are they local, national, or international? Determining their location will set you on the right course for reaching them where they are with what is important to them.

- What words do they use to describe their problem or to look for a solution? When you are writing marketing pieces, emails, correspondence, creating flyers, or the copy for your website, use the terminology your ideal client would use to describe their pain or pleasure point or when looking for a solution.

Coach Kim's Keep It Moving Action Steps:

- Write, draw, or otherwise create an ideal client profile on which every future business decision will be based.

- Determine your ideal client's pain and pleasure points. Review your social media and other marketing mediums to ensure they address your ideal clients' pain and pleasure points.

- Review all of your existing marketing mediums and social media platforms. If they are not target-market friendly, remove or change them.

Key Takeaway

_____

_____

_____

_____

_____

My Next Step

_____

_____

_____

_____

_____

Notes

_____

_____

_____

_____

_____

SECRET #2

Focus on Money Making Activities (MMAs)

Never confuse movement with action

\- Ernest Hemingway

As Ernest Hemingway so eloquently penned, never confuse movement with action. If you want to earn more income in your business, it is important that you focus your energies on Money Making Actions (MMAs) and not just busy work or back office work.

MMAs are the tasks that directly put money in your pocket; for instance, a salesman closing a sale, a landscaper mowing a lawn, or a bookkeeper balancing the books. Delegate as many of the supportive activities as possible, such as administrative tasks and housekeeping. Your MMAs will vary from industry to industry. Take the time to identify your MMAs so you can do more of them and increase your profitability.

In addition to your newfound focus, you will also need perseverance. Many of us do the right thing to increase our profitability, we just don't do it long enough or often enough to make a difference in our bottom-line. Before you give up a course of action, ask yourself the following questions:

- Have I given this project the attention it needs to thrive?
- Have I put in an appropriate amount of effort to see the desired result?
- Is my time best spent somewhere else?
- What are my MMAs (Money Making Activities) and am I focused on them?

- Am I making an emotional decision to discontinue this project based in frustration, fear, etc.?

Coach Kim's Keep It Moving Action Steps:

- Create a written list of your Money Making Activities (MMAs) so you can stay focused on these activities.

- Know and recognize when you slip into your default non-MMA actions. Immediately get back on course by revisiting your MMA list and taking a MMA action step.

- Establish how many MMAs you need to complete daily, weekly, monthly, and annually to meet your income goals and track your progress.

Key Takeaway

_____

_____

_____

_____

_____

My Next Step

_____

_____

_____

_____

_____

Notes

_____

_____

_____

_____

_____

SECRET #3

CHASE ONE RABBIT AT A TIME

Have you ever tried to chase two rabbits at a time? Maybe not. Well, what about two toddlers? You will never catch either one if you try to capture both simultaneously.

In my consulting practice with Catalyst Coaching & Consulting, I have repeatedly seen many entrepreneurs chase more than one rabbit at a time. They mistakenly believe it to be multiple streams of income or Parallel Possibilities, (which I will cover in a later entry) but nothing could be further from the truth. While Parallel Possibilities help you to diversify your offerings and create multiple profit opportunities, multiple rabbits, or unrelated sources, it is actually a division of your resources, time, and energy that will prevent you from increasing your profit margin.

I will never forget one of my business students who was chasing several elusive rabbits. Donna worked hard and was willing to invest in her business. Yet, her profit margin never increased and she could not understand why. Further questions revealed that Donna opened a combination beauty supply/grocery store. Additionally, she also sold some products from a multilevel marketing company. In an effort to cover all bases, she covered none. I tried to explain to her that potential customers were probably confused. After all, if a woman intended to purchase a wig, she probably would not look to purchase it at the grocery store. The product lines were too divergent. The ideal client profile was too dissimilar. Unfortunately for Donna, she did not understand the concept and made a decision to change the name of the store in order to attract customers for all three businesses. Needless to say, this did not work and she never experienced the maximum profit making potential of which she went in search.

Coach Kim's Keep It Moving Action Steps:

- Determine what rabbits (products lines and ideal clients) you are currently chasing.
- Determine whether your rabbits (products lines and business pursuits) are complimentary or if they are too far apart.
- Based on the first two action steps, determine which rabbits you need to let run free and which to pursue
- Once you decide which to pursue, put them in priority order by possibility for profits and ease of implementation. Proceed accordingly.

Key Takeaway

_____

_____

_____

_____

_____

My Next Step

_____

_____

_____

_____

_____

Notes

_____

_____

_____

_____

_____

SECRET #4

PARALLEL POSSIBILITIES: BUILD MULTIPLE PROFIT PLATFORMS

Now that you have learned how to focus on MMAs (Money Making Activities), it is time to diversify your product and service offerings. Parallel Possibilities are the many profit potentials that are birthed out of your original business opportunity - the businesses within the business. Successful entrepreneurs have mastered this concept.

In today's economy, diversification of offerings or multiple profit platforms is the way to survive and thrive. Too many hardworking business owners find their economic brooks drying up with nothing to fall back on. Do not become one of them!

Identify the Parallel Possibilities and other hidden profit sources that will help you to realize the full economic potential of your business. For example, a daycare provider might also consider creating an in-home babysitting service on the weekends or a school holiday care service for elementary school children. The party planner can also sell retail party supplies. Even the publishing company can get in on the action by offering self-publishing consulting and editing services. These are obvious examples but there are many Parallel Possibilities in every industry.

When working with my small business clients, I advise them to create four streams of income - two parallel or complimentary products or services, a residual income source, and a quick hit. I advise you to do the same if you want to finally build the business of your dreams.

Coach Kim's Keep It Moving Action Steps:

- Brainstorm at least ten Parallel Possibilities for your business. Do not screen the ideas for viability at the same time you are brainstorming. Just let your creativity flow.

- Review your list and exclude any Parallel Possibilities that are not complementary to your business and industry.

- Pick two complimentary Parallel Possibilities that you can do most easily and have the largest profit margin to pursue. Put them in place one at a time, giving the first Parallel Possibility the time, energy, effort, and input it needs to thrive before implementing the second. Do not chase too many rabbits at one time, even if they are good rabbits.

Key Takeaway

_____

_____

_____

_____

_____

My Next Step

_____

_____

_____

_____

_____

Notes

_____

_____

_____

_____

_____

SECRET #5

DONUT HOLES

A world famous donut franchise is making millions from selling donut holes. Likewise, donut holes are the smaller opportunities that the larger companies leave behind. Small business owners often make the mistake of trying to compete with the big boys rather than looking for the hidden opportunities that they leave behind.

By way of example, when buyers for a large corporation consider stocking a product, they are thinking in terms of millions. If they are looking for an ROI (return on investment) of $2 million in sales, they won't even consider stocking a product that does not perform at that level, even if it is a great product.

However, for a smaller company, a product selling at that level is a game changer. To the larger company, they might consider this an underperforming product that would create a financial loss. Donut holes may not be as large, but they equally as lucrative.

Coach Kim's Keep It Moving Action Steps:

- Determine if you are offering donuts like everyone else (trying to compete with the "big boys").

- Brainstorm which donut holes you can identify for your products, services, and industry.

- Honestly analyze whether these donut holes are available only because they are not lucrative for the larger firms in your industry.

Key Takeaway

_____

_____

_____

_____

_____

My Next Step

_____

_____

_____

_____

_____

Notes

_____

_____

_____

_____

_____

SECRET #6

RESIDUAL INCOME: SET IT AND FORGET IT (ALMOST)

For a more consistent, constant source of income, create at least one avenue of residual income. Residual income, also known as passive income or royalty income, refers to a product that is created one time and sold in perpetuity. In short, you work hard one time and get paid for it over and over again for the life of the product. Products such as books, e-books, CDs, DVDs, workbooks, home study programs, how-to guides, etc., are great examples. The sky is the limit! This product can be sold on a website or in your retail location. You get paid even if you are not feeling well, on vacation, or pursuing other priorities.

I encourage my consulting clients to maintain the exclusive rights to and creative control of their residual products by self-publishing and production, thus holding the copyright to any audio, written, or video product they produce. While it may initially require more energy, effort and investment, you are able to price as you see fit, enjoy a higher profit margin and maintain artistic control. You will also enjoy greater rewards and more stable income.

Coach Kim's Keep It Moving Action Steps:

- Determine what complementary residual product is best in light of your industry, products, and services.

- Determine what resources you will need to create your residual product, and what you will need to secure these resources. Choose the lowest hanging fruit or easiest to create.

- Look for opportunities to turn existing material into a recorded conference, teleclass, webinar, or the written transcript into an e-book, book, special report, etc.

Key Takeaway

_____

_____

_____

_____

_____

My Next Step

_____

_____

_____

_____

_____

Notes

_____

_____

_____

_____

_____

SECRET #7

QUICK HITS

In addition to Parallel Possibilities and residual income sources, I also encourage my clients to create a Quick Hit. A Quick Hit is your avenue for raising cash quickly. Unexpected emergencies and needs will arise. The savvy entrepreneur protects their profits by planning ahead.

Here are some tips for making a quick hit work for you:

- Remember to utilize products or services on hand. You will not have time to create anything new. Take the path of least resistance.

- Offer gift certificates at a special price for future use for your products or services.
- Have a special price for future services. For example, have clients purchase at a discount in March for use in June. Give the use period an expiration date and schedule that period for your off peak season, days or hours.

Coach Kim's Keep It Moving Action Steps:

- Come up with a product, service, or special project you could offer if you needed an influx of cash in the next several days. Stretch yourself to think beyond borrowing money from your dear Aunt Tilly.

- Plan ahead. Put everything in place you will need to implement a Quick Hit before it is needed. This will enable you to deal with the emergency itself rather than implementing the solution and dealing with an emergency simultaneously.

Key Takeaway

_____

_____

_____

_____

_____

My Next Step

_____

_____

_____

_____

_____

Notes

_____

_____

_____

_____

_____

SECRET #8

PROTECT YOUR PROFITS WITH INSURANCE

Disability Insurance

As an entrepreneur, you cannot call in sick. If you need emergency surgery or time to heal from an injury or other health issue, how will you support yourself and your family? How will you meet your obligations and take care of your responsibilities?

I personally know of a young woman who was the sole financial support of her household. She needed emergency, life-saving surgery. Unfortunately, she did not have disability insurance and spent the three months of her convalescence worried about how she would feed her children and pay her mortgage. She spent the next three years recovering financially. Do not allow this to be your story. A profitable entrepreneur is a responsible, prepared entrepreneur.

Contact your insurance agent, credit union, or other reputable resource to inquire about obtaining disability insurance. It is not as expensive as you may think. It is certainly cheaper than a bankruptcy attorney.

Liability Insurance

Unfortunately, we live in a litigious society. Expect the unexpected. Even well-run businesses can face disaster, litigation, and the unexpected lawsuit. Protect your business by applying for business insurance that covers major property damage and liability. Hopefully you will never need it, but if you do, you will thank me.

Coach Kim's Keep It Moving Action Steps:

- Contact your financial advisor, insurance agent, or banker to discuss your insurance needs.
- Put the appropriate coverage in place as soon as possible. Do not hesitate!
- Notify your significant others and anyone else who would be affected by a loss of your new coverage, where the policies are kept and coverage details.

Key Takeaway

_____

_____

_____

_____

_____

My Next Step

_____

_____

_____

_____

_____

Notes

_____

_____

_____

_____

_____

SECRET #9

DIG A POND: POSITION YOURSELF AS THE EXPERT

Albert Einstein said, "Everybody is a genius. But if you judge a fish by its ability to climb a tree, it will live its whole life believing that it is stupid." I love this quote. I am a firm believer that everyone has a special gift with which they are to bless the world. I am also a firm believer that we are responsible to cultivate and nurture our talents and actively bless others with them.

Have you've heard the expression *become-a-big-fish-in-a-small-pond*? That is what choosing an ideal customer group and becoming an expert is all about. However, I like to take this one step further. You must learn how to rule your pond before you try to conquer the ocean. And if you rule your pond well, I promise you that you will be able to dip your toe into other ponds as well.

We live in an age where specialists rule. Take a look at physicians. Just one generation ago, the same doctor who delivered your baby may also have set your son's broken leg. Today, if you break an arm and a leg you might have two different specialists work with you. And it will probably cost an arm and a leg (pun intended). Why? We compensate people for how much they know on a given subject. The more intricate the knowledge, the more in demand the expert will be and the more they are able to charge.

Accordingly, whenever someone wishes to purchase your products or services they are actually purchasing your expertise, your knowledge, your experience, and your wisdom. You must know your subject matter and industry better than anyone in your circle, or who comes to you either for advice or to make a purchase. People pay for what they do not want to do, do not know how to do, or simply cannot do. If you are not the expert beyond their knowledge, wisdom, and understanding, they have no need for you. They will not see the value of your service or product and they will not make a purchase.

Further, expert positioning becomes its own marketing. Everyone, and I mean everyone, wants to work with the person who is well versed in his or her subject area. Think of the times you needed a referral. Did you seek out the expert or did they come looking for you?

Coach Kim's Keep It Moving Action Steps:

- Learn and use industry-specific terminology and language.
- Establish and build an information databank regarding these subjects and industries for reference.
- Listen to podcasts, join professional associations, attend conferences and workshops, obtain certifications, and read books, blogs, and articles to keep abreast of the latest changes and forthcoming hot button issues in your area of expertise.

Key Takeaway

_____

_____

_____

_____

_____

My Next Step

_____

_____

_____

_____

_____

Notes

_____

_____

_____

_____

_____

SECRET #10

GO FURTHER FASTER: WORK WITH A COACH AND/OR CONSULTANT

While I have seen coaching and consulting referred to interchangeably, they embody totally different skillsets and focuses. Coaches focus on the people behind the business and consultants focus on the processes of the business. In my opinion, you need to address both if you want the strategic advantage that will move you further faster.

By way of explanation, a trained coach will help you to understand what you are called to do, how to create a life you love while doing it, and how to stop self-sabotage by handling the personal issues that prevent your professional success. On the other hand, a consultant brings the specialized education, experience, and expertise needed to diagnose business problems and implement solutions, systems, and processes to create a platform for business success.

While most savvy business owners can readily recognize the need for both a coach and a consultant, it is rare that you can find both skill sets in one person. I strongly believe you will benefit greatly from my dual, hybrid approach to small business coaching and consulting to help you clarify your vision, grow your business, and lead your desired lifestyle.

Coach Kim's Keep It Moving Action Steps:

- Download and complete Coach Kim's *Do You Need a Coach Coachability Index* at http://www.TheCoachKim.com/love-your-life to determine whether you are ready to take advantage of the competitive edge that working with a coach will give you.

- Contact Coach Kim to make an appointment for a one-on-one, personalized laser coaching strategy session at Info@TheCoachKim.com.

- Decide that increasing your profits is worth the investment in your personal and professional growth, and choose a coach and/or consultant that will help you build bigger, faster, and better.

Key Takeaway

_____

_____

_____

_____

_____

My Next Step

_____

_____

_____

_____

_____

Notes

_____

_____

_____

_____

_____

ONE MORE THING
BEFORE YOU GO

I hope these ten profit building secrets have been beneficial to you. Inside of these pages were ideas and tips that I used with many business owners just like you to help them grow their enterprises and make more money. You can have the same experience. However, good ideas only work when you do. The premise behind *Get Paid: 10 Secrets to a Profitable Business* is to give you exactly what you need, in bite-sized pieces so you can be about it, and not just read about it. It is your turn to implement these simple but powerful, profitable strategies.

Now go! And KIM, Keep It Moving toward success!

Blessings and abundance,

Coach Kim

MEET COACH KIM

Kimberly "Coach Kim" Walker, MS, BCC, is the visionary CEO of Catalyst Coaching & Consulting, a business development and personal empowerment firm that specializes in helping motivated entrepreneurs build profitable businesses and lives they love.

Coach Kim has a Master of Science in Organizational Leadership, as well as six certifications as a life and business coach, and is known for her ability to break down complex concepts into achievable actions. An innovative adult educator, dynamic speaker, and insightful business consultant, she offers a fun-filled approach to sound business education for culture, operations, systems, and resources and is highly sought after as a speaker for the business community.

As a life coach, she offers her clients the encouragement, tools, and strategies to build profitable businesses that fully embrace their value system and life priorities.

Get Paid: 10 Secrets to a Profitable Business is her first book.

Keep In Touch With Coach Kim

Facebook   @TheCoachKim

Twitter   @TheCoachKim

Website   www.TheCoachKim.com

Email   Info@TheCoachKim.com

Coming Soon

The MRS Code – Money, Respect, and Sex
www.TheMRSCode.com

Most marriages end due to money troubles. However, for the men who stay in their marriages, they also express dissatisfaction with the respect and sex they receive in the relationship. I help married men gain more satisfaction in all three.

I coach husbands to enjoy a higher quality of life by helping them to increase their incomes through entrepreneurship, to become the man they always knew they could be through character development, and enjoy a higher quality and quantity sex life.

Register at www.TheMRSCode.com to be the first to hear all the latest news and updates! Take this important first step to making the rest of your life the best of your life!

The VIP Virtual Coaching Group with Coach Kim

Registration is open to a limited group of people who are serious about growing their businesses. We have some big opportunities you won't want to miss!

The VIP Virtual Coaching Group is perfect for people who want to make more money in their business and live a life they love. It is designed to help people to move forward faster. Because of the internet, we can now meet together and it doesn't matter where you're located or your time zone.

Your VIP Virtual Coaching Group membership includes:

- Virtual coaching meetings with Coach Kim
- LIVE calls with Coach Kim and the coaching group
- Action steps you can take in your business
- Templates to simplify your systems
- Interaction with Coach Kim in her private Facebook group
- Recordings of all virtual meetings for your learning library you can have forever
- Special guest experts from around the world
- Resources to help you build faster and stronger than ever before
- Ask Coach Kim questions on her Q & A day where she'll take any question on any topic you'd like

Some of the topics the VIP Coaching Group will include:

- Build your legacy
- Leverage your strategic relationships
- Identify multiple streams of income
- Become an expert
- Residual income creation
- Stop being busy and start being productive
- Strategic business planning
- Low cost marketing
- Video trainings
- Life planning
- Achieving work/life balance
- Business assessments from Coach Kim personally
- …and much, much more!

To register or to get more information check out www.TheCoachKim.com/coaching-group.